Know About Shivaji

MAPLE KIDS

KNOW ABOUT SHIVAJI

ALL RIGHTS RESERVED. No part of this book may be reproduced in a retrieval system or transmitted in any form or by any means electronics, mechanical, photocopying, recording and or without permission of the publisher.

Published by

MAPLE PRESS PRIVATE LIMITED
office: A-63, Sector 58, Noida 201301, U.P., India
phone: +91 120 455 3581, 455 3583
email: info@maplepress.co.in
website: www.maplepress.co.in

Reprinted in 2019

ISBN: 978-93-50334-13-3

Contents

Preface 5
1. Birth of a Legend 6
2. Early Years 9
3. Youth and Marriage 13
4. Jijabai 16
5. The Making of the Warrior 19
6. The Siege of Toranagadh 22
7. The Diplomat 24
8. Afzal Khan 27
9. The Victory 30
10. The Narrow Escape 34
11. Baji Prabhu 37
12. The Defeat of Shaista Khan 40
13. Shivaji and Aurangzeb 43
14. Flight from Prison 46
15. At Raigadh 49
16. Shivaji and Guru Ramdas 51
17. Coronation 55
18. Shivaji - The Emperor 58
19. The Reformer 62
20. More Reforms 65
21. Shivaji - The Man 69
22. Successors of Shivaji 72
23. Remembering Shivaji 74
24. Timeline of Shivaji 77

Preface

Shivaji, the first Chhatrapati of the Maratha Empire, is known for his legendary accomplishments, just administration and military expertise. Shivaji was not only the maker of Maratha Empire, but also the greatest constructive genius of medieval India. States fell, empires broke up, dynasties became extinct, but the memory of a true 'hero and king', like Shivaji, remains an imperishable historical legacy for an entire human race.

This book is a biography of Shivaji who clearly outstands most rulers and generals of India by his exemplary life and is thus respected by the entire cross-section of Indians. Shivaji holds the same importance in India as Napoleon to Europe.

Chapter 1
Birth of a Legend

Shivaji Bhonsle is worshipped as the father of 'the Maratha nation' in Maharashtra. He was born in 1627, in a family of Maratha officials. His father, Shahaji, was the *jagirdar* of the Sultan of Ahmednagar in Pune, and his mother was Jijabai.

A story revolves around the birth of Shivaji. One night, Shahaji had a dream where a sanyasi gave him a mango

and said, "You and your wife should eat it. Soon you will have a son who will become very great."

When Shahaji awoke, he was surprised to see a real mango in his hand. The dream felt real as if Lord Shiva himself, instructed him through his dream. He partly ate the mango and gave the rest to Jijabai.

Soon after that incident, they were blessed with a son. Shahaji named him Shivaji, as his birth was foretold by Lord Shiva himself.

Soon after the birth of Shivaji, his father shifted his loyalty to the Sultan of Bijapur. This was not the first time that Shahaji shifted his loyalties. When the Mughal emperor Shah Jahan had decided to lead his forces into the Deccan, Shahaji had accepted the offer of a *mansabdari* from the emperor. However, upon the emperor's retreat in 1632, once again, Shahaji decided to accept the domain of the Sultan of Ahmednagar. But he was taken captive by the Sultan of Bijapur as the agreement signed by the Sultan of Ahmednagar was no longer valid.

With his father exiled from Pune, Shivaji was raised in the city. The city not only became the capital of Maratha power, but also the seat of real and imagined Hindu martial traditions.

The early six years of Shivaji's life made him grow in highly unsettled conditions. Nevertheless, his mother, Jijabai, made sure that his education was not neglected. She was a devoted mother. She instilled in him the qualities that a king should adhere, and a fierce faith in *'Dev'* (God), *'Desh'* (Country) and *'Dharma'* (Deeds). At a tender age, she read to him stories of Rama, Arjun, Krishna and other heroes in the epics. In the later years, he grew up as a valiant warrior.

CHAPTER 2
Early Years

When Shivaji first came to Pune, he was pleased to see the huge Shivneri peaks at a distance. They reminded him of his childhood days when he used to play on the soils of the Shivneri fort. Present day Pune is very different from those days. Earlier it was situated on the banks of Mutha River and was known as Punavdi.

But unfortunately when Shivaji arrived in Pune, there were signs of destruction everywhere. The enemies of Shahaji had destroyed the entire township, which was once so well-maintained and neat. The entire township was covered with broken houses, temples and destroyed property. People fled away in fear. Neglected and uncultivated fields turned into wilderness. Such was the state of the town!

Environment plays a vital role in shaping the character of the child. It is aptly proved by none other than the life of Shivaji. He was born at a time when the Hindus were totally defeated at the hands of Muslims. As a witness, he vowed to stand against the Muslims rule. He promised

to free his beloved motherland from the claws of the foreigners.

It was a relief for the people in the neighboring villages when they heard that Shivaji and Jijabai had made Pune their home. Slowly, the inhabitants started to come back and the city gradually lost its deserted look.

When Jijabai and Shivaji came to Pune, they were accompanied by a loyal escort called Dadaji Kond Dev. In the latter years, he took up the role as Shivaji's teacher. He was also supposed to look after the two and manage the Jagir.

Dadaji was strict and a just disciplinarian. He was also a faithful servant of Shahaji Bhonsle and Jijabai. Shivaji was the apple of his eye.

Shivaji's education continued under the supervision of Dadaji. As time passed, he became an expert horseman.

He acquired great skill in spear throwing, archery, '*dand-patta*' and wrestling. He also learned how to run the *jagir*. Frequently, he would go around the *jagir* with Dadaji and learn how it was administered. In the presence of Shivaji, Dadaji settled disputes and even awarded punishments.

These in turn made Shivaji learn how to win people's hearts and deliver necessary justice.

Shivaji travelled around Maval in the company of Dadaji. People living in this area were known as 'Mavalis'. They were loyal, hard working and quick-footed. They were tired of getting harassed by the Sultan's rule. Shivaji felt the need to do something about the situation. He asked for his mother's opinion to which she replied, "Make your subjects happy". These words were enough to inspire young Shivaji. He aspired to become courageous and brave like the heroes in the past.

As a child, Shivaji used to play with the poor children in the neighborhood. He even visited their huts and shared their simple meal comprising of onion and "*Bhakri*', a type of Roti, with great relish. They invented games to pass their time. Shivaji joined the Mavalis in the games and became quite popular among them.

Likewise, the early years of Shivaji were spent under the loving care of Dadaji and Jijabai.

CHAPTER 3
Youth and Marriage

Shahaji Bhonsle's *jagir* was undergoing a transformation at that time. Under the guidance of Dadaji, Shivaji made the Mavalis realise the concept of Swaraj.

Shivaji was to rule the Pune *jagir* then, and Shahaji Bhonsle gladly handed over the *jagir* and made the necessary arrangements.

When Shivaji was fourteen years old, Jijabai started thinking of his marriage. So, she started looking for a suitable wife for Shivaji and soon found the girl she was

looking for. Her name was Saibai and she came from the Nimbalkar family of Phalthan, near Pune. The marriage was celebrated with great splendor at their palace.

Shivaji and his band of Marathas claimed to have originated the idea of guerrilla warfare in India. For a good many years, they plundered the countryside, and Shivaji came to acquire an inspiring reputation as a warrior. But, Shivaji's main motive lay in defeating Bijapur.

Prior to this, on a certain occasion, Shahaji took his son

to the court of the Sultan of Bijapur. Shivaji was not even twelve years of age. As a gesture of respect, Shahaji touched the ground thrice and saluted the Sultan and asked his son to follow. But, Shivaji retreated a few steps. He stood erect with his head unbent. His demeanor reflected his determination to not bow down to any foreign ruler. He retreated from the court with a lion-like gait and bearing.

Not a single soul had ever dared to behave in such a manner at the court of the Sultan of Bijapur. All were wonder-struck at the boldness of the young boy.

But instead of getting enraged, Shahaji was mighty pleased at heart. Though he had not been fortunate enough to be an independent ruler, he sent his son to Pune to let him shape into one such ruler.

Without any doubt, the person who instilled the first lesson in valour and uprightedness in Shivaji was none other than his mother, Jijabai.

CHAPTER 4
Jijabai

The story of Shivaji is incomplete without the story of Jijabai.

Jijabai, the mother of Shivaji, was an epitome of self-respect. In those times, she was both the protector of the country and her religion. She guided and shaped Shivaji's mind from his early years. Jijabai had taught her son the values and courage to fight for Hindu sovereignty by telling him stories from the great Hindu epics, the Ramayana and the Mahabharata. Jijabai took great steps to ensure that Shivaji grew up in an environment favorable enough to build his character.

Shahaji, her husband, lived in Bangalore. Taking his permission, she moved to Pune and lived under the guardianship of Dadaji Khond Dev. She shifted because she felt that the luxurious lifestyle in Bangalore would not be suitable to build Shivaji's moral and physical strength. Jijabai's shaping of Shivaji's character began when he was still in her womb. At that time, Jijabai prayed to Goddess Bhavani to bless her with a good son. Even when he was

in her womb, she had apprised Shivaji of his objective to become the protector of cows and Brahmins and initiate the motivating force of the Hindu Rashtra.

Jijabai not only inspired Shivaji in his struggle, but also guided him on every step on his way to victory, through her brilliance and commitment. The following incident truly conveys her sentiments.

Shivaji and Jijamata were playing *chausar*, or chess. Suddenly, Shivaji asked, "What are the terms for victory?" Looking out of the window, Jijamata pointed to the green flag fluttering atop the fort at Kondana and said, "On our victory the color of that flag would change". In his later years, he shaped it as his mission and was able to accomplish it to victory. Jijabai not only inspired Shivaji, but also gave him lessons on strategy and planning. Shivaji was attacked by Afzal Khan with a large army. Jijabai made him aware that Afzal Khan would not fight by the rules as she still remembers how Afzal Khan had killed Sambhaji through fraudulent means. This piece of advice enabled Shivaji to defeat such a powerful enemy like Afzal Khan.

There were many such endeavors and trials. But Jijamata never allowed any of these to hinder her son's path for self-rule. Shivaji highly revered his mother and asked for her advice on every important decision of his life.

CHAPTER 5
The Making of the Warrior

As time passed, Shivaji began to openly display his rejection of the Muslim rule. Meanwhile, his fame as a courageous young man had reached far and wide. He was equally admired by both Hindus and Muslims.

Gradually, Shivaji began to oppose some of the livelihood preferences of the Muslims. He greatly disliked the Muslim's practice of killing and eating of the holy cow. He began to despise the butchers who sold cow's meat. With the permission of the Sultan, he banned the slaughtering of cows.

But once, a butcher ignored the Sultan's orders and sat at the city gates to sell a basketful of meat. Shivaji was passing that way with his friend. Seeing this, he jumped down from his horse, drew his sword and beheaded the butcher. Such was his anger. But later, he realized and repented for such a hasty action.

He began to think of ways of overthrowing the foreign rule. He knew that this would be possible only when he

❖ Know About Shivaji ❖

would fully prepare himself as a warrior, and soon the task began.

Shivaji spent most of his days and nights in the jungles of the Western Ghats. He toiled hard to train himself in climbing mountains and walking through dense forests. He gathered courage and skills to defend him against wild animals. After spending sometime in the Western Ghats, he returned back to his mother. He told her about his idea of leading an army of Mavalis. Hearing this, his mother warned him against the backwardness of Mavalis. But he noticed no such difference as according to him, they lived on the same land as he does and therefore they are all one. His mother was pleased on hearing him and gave her consent.

The first and foremost thing that was on Shivaji's mind was to free his region from the hands of Bijapur and its Sultan. The Mavalis, without any doubt, proved themselves as loyal soldiers who could be trained for his army. He picked several Mavali deshmukhs as he travelled, who lead different Mavali tribes. Through them, he appealed to his army of Mavalis to oppose the Muslims. They agreed to everything he said hypnotized by the young soldiers' zeal.

CHAPTER 6
The Siege of Toranagadh

After the initial preparation, Shivaji planned to win Toranagadh or the Fort of Torana.

Shivaji brought the chiefs together and informed them of capturing Toranagadh soon. Together, they planned for a war. They targeted to convince the Governor of Torana that Shivaji had prior orders from Bijapur to take charge over it. In order to do so, Shivaji gave him a bag of gold and convinced him. He thus, captured the fort of Torana in 1646. This was the first siege led by Shivaji.

After Toranagadh, Shivaji began capturing forts. This news of Shivaji's conquests reached the Sultan of Bijapur. In order to crush Shivaji, he hatched a plan. He got Shahaji captured by false means. Shahaji was then brought to the Sultan's presence and was thrown into the prison. The rumor of Shahaji torture and execution spread across town.

Shivaji, who was rejoicing in the birth of an era of independence, was deeply struck by this news. His mother, Jijabai was heartbroken. She felt as if the God of Death was snatching her sacred '*mangalya*', the symbol of life-long partnership with the husband. Along with this, Shivaji was attacked with a series of bad news. Firstly, Fateh Khan, the valiant Sardar of Bijapur, was proceeding against Shivaji with a large army. Secondly, Farrad Khan, yet another valiant general; attacked Sambhaji, the elder brother of Shivaji. Evidently, the Sultan was posing these threats to force Shivaji to give up fighting and surrender. It was a clear that if he did not surrender, his father's life would be in danger. Shivaji was worried and confused.

Finding him in such a dilemma, his fourteen-year-old wife, Saibai, said, "Why do you worry yourself over this? Make sure that your father is free and also see to it that you still maintain this state of independence. Destroy your enemies." Needless to say, she was the worthy wife of a hero like Shivaji.

CHAPTER 7

The Diplomat

Like a true diplomat, Shivaji made a decision. He decided to deal with Fateh Khan first. The Sultan of Bijapur employed the commander of Purandaragadh. Shivaji won his heart with his politeness. He stationed a small army there. The soldiers of Shivaji fought against Fateh Khan who attacked the fort. This was the first attempt towards their battle for independence. Fateh Khan retreated and ran away, seeing the valiancy of Shivaji's army. Elsewhere, Sambhaji was also able to defeat Farrad Khan.

He successfully dealt with the attacks, but how was he to save his father? Shivaji was deeply troubled. Suddenly, he struck a plan. Shah Jahan was the Emperor in Delhi at that time. Shivaji wrote to the Emperor, "My father is kept captive by the Sultan of Bijapur. As soon as he is released, I will willingly serve you. We are very eager."

The Sultan of Bijapur came to know of Shivaji's appeal to Shah Jahan. He was aware that the Emperor of Delhi was waiting for an opportunity to attack him. He feared that the combined forces of the Emperor and Shivaji

would attack him at any moment. This led to the release of Shahaji with due honour. With such valour and diplomacy, Shivaji overcame the first great danger to freedom.

Shivaji was now twenty-eight. By this time Kondana, Purandara, Kalyan, Raigadh and almost forty forts, waved the flag of Shivaji's freedom.

But, Shivaji did not rest. He was worried about the upcoming troubles on the state as the English, the Portuguese and other foreigners had already set their foot on the West Coast. Shivaji foresaw the dominance and unsuspected dangers from these foreign armies, who might one day, occupy the whole land. He immediately started preparing and ensured measures to check such an invasion. In order to oppose them, he began building fortresses by the sea. He also furnished himself with warships, and trained the navy.

CHAPTER 8
Afzal Khan

Sultan Adilshah of Bijapur was anxious and helpless as he saw Shivaji's dream of Swaraj coming true. Almost every day he was flooded with one or more news of Shivaji's conquests and victories!

The Sultan had an adoptive mother, Uliya Begum who hated Shivaji.

One day, she held a Durbar. All the far-famed heroes of Bijapur attended it. At that Durbar, Uliya Begum threw out a challenge to those present, "if there is one amongst you who can capture and bring Shivaji as a captive, let him accept this token gift of *pan*." Saying this, she held out the ceremonial '*pan*' and betel-nut offering placed on a silver platter. The general, Afzal Khan came forward and accepted the challenge. He was robust, tall and cruelly deceitful. The Sultan extended his help by sending a force of 25,000 soldiers to help him in his mission.

Afzal Khan planned to destroy Bhavani of Tuljapur, the family deity worshipped by Shivaji. His axe broke several

idols of Goddess Bhavani to pieces. Shivaji was informed of these happenings.

Afzal Khan knew his inability to defeat Shivaji as long as he was behind his fortresses in the jungle areas. He wished Shivaji to fight with him out in the open. To anger him, he desecrated temples, slaughtered cows and even molested women. He thought this to be an easier way to defeat Shivaji.

Shivaji began to understand the scheme. He knew that he would be easily overpowered, if he came out of his forts and declared battle. So, he decided to proceed to the new fort of Pratapagadh, which he had built in the forest of Javali. He then planned to attract Afzal Khan to this place, and defeat him there. At this time, he had a dream. In this dream, Goddess Bhavani appeared and blessed him to be victorious.

CHAPTER 9
The Victory

Soon, Afzal Khan thought of a plan to make Shivaji come out of his fort of Pratapagadh and meet him on the plains. So, he sent his representative with some secret instructions. He met Shivaji and politely informed him that Afzal Khan was a great friend of his father and that he did not intend any harm and requested Shivaji to come down to meet him. Using his wit, Shivaji also sent a flattering letter through his own representative. He wrote, "As we are a family, I request you to forgive all my crimes. You should come to Pratapagadh, uplift and take me to the Sultan of Bijapur." The humble and pleading tone of Shivaji's letter mislead Afzal Khan. Shivaji's representative praised the courage of the Khan and made fun of Shivaji's lack of courage. Afzal Khan was immensely pleased.

His forces accompanied Afzal Khan to the forest of Javali. He stationed himself right at the foot of Pratapagadh. As decided, this was supposed to be a friendly encounter. It was also agreed that as Shivaji was a little terrified, Afzal

Khan should meet Shivaji alone. Even the bodyguards of both the parties should remain at some distance.

Just a night before this meeting, no one was able to sleep. Netaji, Tanaji, Kanoji and other trusted lieutenants of Shivaji came down from the fort, and hid in the forest

with their battalions. They stood ready in action. They were instructed that they should fall upon the enemy tanks and destroy them the moment they heard the booming cannon on the fort. The day dawned. As usual, Shivaji bathed and worshipped Lord Shiva. He put on a metallic helmet to protect the head and a metallic cast to protect his chest. He had the dagger 'Bhavani' and a sharp knife attached to the scabbard of his waist. He prayed to Goddess Bhavani and went down the fort to meet Afzal Khan. They were to meet halfway down the hill. The place was hidden from the view of the camp of Afzal Khan. In the *shamiana* or tent shelter, Afzal waited for Shivaji. He rose as soon as he saw Shivaji. Their eyes met for a while. Pretending to offer him the customary embrace of friendship, Khan invited Shivaji, and stretched both his arms. The embrace itself seemed fatal. Shivaji came forward and embraced him. Unexpectedly, Afzal Khan with all his deceit and cruelty stabbed Shivaji on his side. Shivaji's steel vest tore making a grating noise. Shivaji quickly released himself from the hold of the Khan. He dragged out his own knife and thrust it deep into the entrails of Afzal Khan. The Khan tried to run away. But Shivaji flung his sword at him and beheaded him at one stroke.

Shivaji stuck the severed head of the Khan on his sword and ran up to the fort. Simultaneously, the cannon boomed and seemed to cut open the skies. Hearing the cannon, the Khan's soldiers rejoiced, thinking of Afzal's victory against

Shivaji. Suddenly, the soldiers of Shivaji pounced upon them like leopards and completely destroyed them. At this moment, Goddess Tulaja Bhavani was fully avenged. Shivaji was all-victorious. He sent Jijabai a gift. The gift was the head of Afzal Khan!

CHAPTER 10
The Narrow Escape

Shivaji's fame as a killer of Afzal Khan had spread everywhere in the country and abroad. This news left the Sultan of Bijapur in dismay. Even at this moment of victory, Shivaji was highly focused. Taking advantages of this state, he proceeded to other places and captured quite a few forts of the Sultan of Bijapur.

The Sultan of Bijapur chose another general and sent him to attack Shivaji, this time with a stronger force of seventy thousand. The general, Siddi Jauhar, tried his best to equip himself so as to capture Shivaji who was in Panhalgadh. He was assisted by the English assisted with their artillery. The attack gathered more and more strength. Shivaji was disappointed when the attack did not lose its force even after the monsoons set in. At the same time, as requested by the Sultan of Bijapur, the Badshah of Delhi sent his uncle Shaista Khan with an army of a hundred thousand soldiers to attack Shivaji. All hopes for Swaraj and survival seemed to die out.

During this crucial period, Shivaji's mother Jijabai took up her son's charge of the administration and ably managed the affairs.

In the meantime, Shivaji decided that he should free himself from these encirclements. He had to find a way as Siddi Jauhar was guarding the fort from below. Shivaji thought for an alternative way to escape. He planned to send an envoy to Siddi Jauhar, with a proposal to surrender. He appealed that he would surrender unconditionally the very next day and should be pardoned. The news of this surrender filled the soldiers in merriment. They hardly knew that such letters from Shivaji were too sweet to be true. It rained heavily that night with terrible thunder and lightning. At that moment, Shivaji along with 800 of his men got down the fort and proceeded stealthily towards

Vishagadh. The soldiers posted to watch the enemies were in their tents, but they were lost in merriment, thinking of Shivaji's surrender. Even a slightest suspicion would have caused utter destruction. Hence Shivaji's men were cautious at every step. But, they had Bhavani's blessings with them. They were able to escape unnoticed.

CHAPTER 11
Baji Prabhu

Destiny had other plans for Shivaji. No matter how fast the group of Mavali soldiers carrying Shivaji in a palanquin ran, they still got noticed by one of the spies of Siddi Jauhar during a large streak of lightening. Siddi Jauhar was immediately informed of this escape.

Jauhar was dumbstruck after getting the news, but did not lose heart. He sent for his son-in-law Siddi Masood. He was entrusted with the cavalry and was sent to pursue Shivaji. Even Shivaji felt that it would be difficult to escape this time. But he immediately devised a plan. He

sat in another palanquin which travelled in a different direction. There was a man in the army who looked like Shivaji. He was made to wear the clothes of Shivaji and sat in the first palanquin. The enemy soldiers captured him and proceeded to Siddi Jauhar. But when the captive was questioned, it was found that he was not Shivaji but a barber of Panhalgadh! All were put to shame.

This time, Siddi Masood decided to take up the chase. Shivaji and his soldiers had already covered a distance of twenty-five miles. They were about to reach Vishalgadh and were near the valley of Gajapur. They were attacked by five thousands soldiers of Masood. Baji Prabhu Deshpande was Shivaji's lieutenant. He established as an epitome of loyalty when he requested Shivaji to proceed to Vishalgadh with half of the army. He was an embodiment of strength and bravery. With the remaining half he faced the mighty battle with Siddi Masood. It was an epic sight to see Baji Prabhu wielding two swords in both his hands.

In that narrow valley, Baji Prabhu began cutting and defeating the Pathan soldiers. The battle wounded him terribly and blood was oozing out. Nevertheless, he bravely fought the battle till evening. Many of his soldiers were also wounded and dead. Even after such fierce bravery, Baji Prabhu fell as a victim to an enemy's sword that severely wounded him. At the same time, Shivaji overpowered the soldiers who were attacking Vishalgadh, climbed up the fort and let the cannon resound his victory. Hearing this sound, Baji Prabhu died in peace, happy that his efforts for his master were not wasted in vain. The blood of such a martyr made the valley sacred. Hence, this valley came to be known as Pavan Khind or the Sacred Valley.

CHAPTER 12
The Defeat of Shaista Khan

The news of Shivaji's escape from Panhalgadh fell in the ears of the Sultan of Bijapur. He felt like he had been struck by a thousand thunderbolts at once. He lost all his courage to summon again and attack Shivaji. But, Shivaji had other dangers from Shaista Khan to attend to. For this, he chose the month of Ramzan which is regarded sacred to the Muslims. This was an ideal time as the community fasted all day, then ate sumptuously and was fast asleep at night.

The day also marked the anniversary of the crowning of Aurangzeb. On that day the Muslim soldiers were absorbed in revelry and merriment of a great feast. Shivaji chose this day to come down from Raigadh with an army of two thousand soldiers. He stationed himself at a distance of some two miles from Pune. Shaista Khan was then camping in the Lal Mahal at Pune. It was in this Mahal where Shivaji was brought up as a boy. A hundred thousand soldiers of the Mughal Emperor were stationed in and around Pune.

Babaji, a childhood friend of Shivaji, moved towards the Mughal camp with a small force of soldiers. Behind him, Shivaji proceeded with another small troop. Babaji entered the city, chatting and shouting. The sentries stopped him and his men.

Without much hesitation, he called themselves as Khan's men and clarified that they had gone for a watch and were now returning back. He and his men disregarded the sentries and quietly entered the city. Shivaji's soldiers followed them. Entering through the rear gates of the Lal Mahal, he went to the kitchen and killed everyone present there. Then he proceeded to Shaista Khan's bedroom where he was fast asleep. He pulled down a small wall that obstructed his entry. A servant heard the sound and went to inform the Khan. But nevertheless, the Khan was so deep in his sleep that he drove the servant away saying that it must be some rat in the kitchen.

Shivaji and his men rushed in. By that time, the entire Lal Mahal filled with shouts which announced that the enemy had broken in. Wives of Shaista Khan hid him behind a curtain. Shivaji burst in and flung his sword. Three fingers of the Khan, one for each of the three syllables in the name 'Shivaji', were chopped off by this throw.

The Khan jumped down from the window. By then, the Mughal army had already surrounded the Lal Mahal. In utter confusion, Shivaji and his men shouted, "Catch the enemy, cut him into pieces!"

They escaped to Simhaoadh after opening the doors of the Lal Mahal. This incident convinced the enemies of Shivaji that he shouldn't be misinterpreted as 'a mountain rat', but was some sort of a friend or demon with superhuman powers. Aurangzeb was put to unbearable shame and transferred Shaista Khan to Bengal as a punishment.

CHAPTER 13
Shivaji and Aurangzeb

The consecutive victories of Shivaji led to many other problems. The foremost was the collection of finances. Shivaji knew that he needed huge finances in order to independently build up such a vast kingdom well-equipped with an army and navy. He targeted Aurangzeb, who was considered as one of the wealthiest rulers of the country.

In those days Surat was known as the city of Kubera, the God of Wealth. So on one occasion, he attacked Surat and emptied the entire city. This incident highly angered Aurangzeb and he lost his patience.

But unlike others, he did not lead an army against Shivaji. He was well aware of the capabilities of Shivaji. So, he thought of a plan. He decided to send King Raja Jayasimha to overpower Shivaji. Jayasimha was a great warrior and a hero. He was also a clever general.

Jayasimha proceeded south with his large army. Due to his past enmity with Shivaji, the Sultan of Bijapur assisted

Jayasimha. The battle against Shivaji began. Suddenly, Shivaji wrote a letter to Jayasimha proposing a friendly compromise. He even met Jayasimha and told him that he would remain loyal to the Badshah of Delhi.

Shivaji's decision of surrendering without fighting baffled everyone. He was thought to be as brave as a lion, grown independently in the mountain ranges of Sahyadri. It was also possible that Shivaji would go to Delhi on the pretext of serving the Badshah but then would put an end to the life of Aurangzeb. This was perhaps a venture that needed greater heroism and sharper strategy than ever before.

Accordingly, Shivaji proceeded to meet the Emperor, Aurangzeb. His son, Sambhaji, also accompanied him. His home was filled with great anxiety. As he proceeded, the Hindu community welcomed him and bowed down to him respectfully. Shivaji reached Agra in order to meet Aurangzeb. The latter was equally tactful. He did not let Shivaji approach him. He bid him to stay at a distance in the court.

CHAPTER 14

Flight from Prison

The way Shivaji was treated highly disappointed him. Aurangzeb acted in a way that insulted him. Shivaji was angry as Aurangzeb failed to keep his promise of treating him with respect. Ignoring Aurangzeb, he left the court.

Shivaji was now in great danger. Aurangzeb was not a fool to let an enemy, who had come within his reach, to escape so easily. He ordered Shivaji to be imprisoned and executed.

Shivaji was now in prison at the orders of the Mughal Emperor. But, Shivaji did not lose patience and began to plan his escape from the prison. At such a critical hour, his intellect and courage shone more brightly. Suddenly Shivaji fell ill. His condition grew worse. In such a state, Shivaji begged Aurangzeb to allow his Maratha soldiers to return. Aurangzeb felt relieved and permitted them to go. Shivaji distributed sweets to the Fakirs, mendicants and ascetics of the town, so as to cure his illness. He began sending gifts to the wealthy in the town. He did everything with Aurangzeb's permission. Even, a clever ruler like

Aurangzeb failed to foresee the plans that Shivaji had in mind. No '*vaidya*' or '*hakim*' could improve Shivaji's condition. The date was fixed for Shivaji's execution. A day before the execution, Shivaji's condition grew worse, and he lost his consciousness.

As per the schedule, the baskets to carry the sweets were brought in. As planned, Shivaji and his son suddenly jumped into one of the baskets. Immediately, the servants put on the lids and carried the baskets away.

The sentries, who examined the baskets, were convinced by the long custom that they contained nothing but sweets. Some of the baskets came under the supervision of the chief of the sentries, Polad Khan, but they contained merely sweets. Luckily, the Khan did not examine the baskets in which Shivaji and Sambhaji were

hidden. Partly by the grace of Goddess Bhavani and partly due to Khan's forgetfulness, Shivaji escaped.

Inside the prison, in the place of Shivaji, a friend of his, Hiroji lay down. He wore the royal ring to be mistaken as Shivaji. He lay down with his hand on his forehead which showed this ring thrust out. The rest of his body was covered with a blanket. Madari, an innocent looking lad, kept massaging Hiroji's limbs. Polad Khan peeped in now and then to keep a check on Shivaji.

Finally, the day came to a close and it was nightfall. Hiroji pretending to be 'Shivaji' got up and arranged the blankets and the pillows to make it look like a man sleeping on the couch. Putting on his usual clothes, he came out and announced to the sentries that the condition of Shivaji was very serious and that it was a matter of a few hours for Shivaji. He went out to bring some medicines. Madari also quietly followed him. Both went away never to return. Inside, on the couch, laid the imitated Shivaji. His cell was guarded by sentries with their swords drawn.

The day of Shivaji's execution dawned. Polad Khan came in. There was a strange silence. He grew suspicious. As he stepped in, he found 'Shivaji' asleep. For a moment, this sight brought some comfort to his heart. Suddenly he noticed that there was no movement. He grew suspicious and pulled back the blanket.

He was astonished to find a bare bed and pillows in place of Shivaji! He was surprised at Shivaji's ability to vanish under such strict supervision.

CHAPTER 15
At Raigadh

Aurangzeb's anger knew no bounds when he heard about the flight of Shivaji from prison. Aurangzeb at once ordered his army to capture Shivaji, and his army was set out in all directions.

By this time, Shivaji and Sambhaji had already mounted the horses that were ready for them, and had proceeded south. They dashed away at a great speed. On the way, they took shelter at the *Maths* established by Swami Samarth Ramdas. He inspired Shivaji and Shivaji became his disciple thereafter. Dressed as a '*sanyasi*', Shivaji finally reached Raigadh. For a while, even his mother Jijabai could not recognize him. But, when she did, his return filled her heart with joy and pride to have given birth to such a noble son.

The news of Shivaji's escape from Agra made his enemies in the South speechless and helpless. Shivaji's fame spread all over India. The great Maratha hero successfully threw dust into the eyes of the greatest plotter and politician like Aurangzeb. He managed to escape from the Emperor's capital, where he was kept under twenty-four hours invigilation of the sentries who stood with their swords drawn. The world had never witnessed such a daring act of cleverness.

CHAPTER 16
Shivaji and Guru Ramdas

Guru Ramdas was one of the greatest saints of the world. He was the Guru of Shivaji in the real sense. He was also a great devotee of Hanuman and Lord Rama.

It has already been mentioned that Ramdas was the helper of Shivaji in his cause to liberate India.

It was believed that Lord Rama had himself instructed his devotee Ramdas to aid Shivaji for the noble cause. Starting from river Krishna, the Guru went on preaching from Mahabaleshwar to Kolhapur. The eleven principal seats of Maruti established by him emphasized the importance of physical development. He helped to put up the shrines of Sri Ramachandra at Champavati and introduced Sri Rama Navami Mahotsava with the procession of Sri Rama's chariot. It was in Singanvadi that Shivaji became the disciple of Ramdas.

When Shivaji became the king of Maharashtra, he placed the sandals of his Guru on the throne. He acted as the governor of the kingdom working under the orders and guidance of his Guru. He adopted the flag of orange to

❖ Know About Shivaji ❖

ensign his reign. A beautiful story follows about Shivaji's adoption of the '*Gerua*' flag and his ruling of the kingdom in the name of Saint Ramdas. The story goes as follows.

One day, from the terrace of his palace, Shivaji saw Gurudev Ramdas going about the streets with a begging bowl. Shivaji couldn't understand the need to beg when he had already placed all his resources at the feet of his Gurudev. Shivaji called his companion Balaji. He wrote a small letter and asked him to give it to Guruji when he came to the palace.

At noon, Ramdas came to the palace with his bowl and Balaji bowed down before Gurudev and placed the letter at his feet. The letter briefly conveyed that Shivaji had gifted his entire kingdom to Gurudev and humbly begged for his Gurudev's blessing. The Guru smiled and told Balaji that it was all right. Next morning, Ramdas called Shivaji and asked him what he proposed to do with himself as he had disposed off his kingdom.

Shivaji bowed down before Ramdas and said that he would be very happy and would consider himself blessed, if he could spend his life in his Gurudev's service. To this Ramdas replied, "Take this bowl and let us go on our rounds". Without a second thought, Shivaji did as he was told. In sheer admiralty and reverence, people bowed and gave them alms. The pair returned to the river. Ramdas prepared simple meals and Shivaji partook of what was left after his Gurudev had finished his meals. Unable to

hold his curiosity, Shivaji asked the purpose behind such a practice. Ramdas knew that the opportunity had come to set up a grand ideal for the king. Ramdas asked Shivaji to rule the kingdom in his (Ramdas') name, take the *Gerua chaddar* for his banner and defend its honour with his life. This would enable him to think that the kingdom did not belong to him, to treat it as a trust to be ruled justly and well before God. Thus, the *Gerua banner* was decided to ensign Shivaji's rule.

During his lifetime, Ramdas sent his disciples to all parts of India to preach and spread the Hindu religion. His disciples and Mutts in the North directly or indirectly helped Shivaji in his work. Ramdas' organization in the South, in Thanjavur, helped Shivaji's son, Rajaram, to go to Jinji and carry on the twenty years' war with Aurangzeb.

CHAPTER 17

Coronation

Though Shivaji had, by 1670, recaptured many of the fortresses he had previously surrendered to Aurangzeb, he still wasn't approved by the Mughal Emperor to be entitled as 'Raja'. His application was granted in 1668. Shivaji's coronation in 1674 as Chhatrapati, or the 'Lord of the Universe', constituted the most important chapter in his life. It was reported that 11,000 Brahmins under Gaga Bhatta's guidance chanted the Vedas, and around 50,000 men were present at the coronation ceremony, which concluded with the chants "Shivaji Maharaj-ki jai!"

His coronation marked his independence from the Mughals, and rejected any kind of formal relation to them. Even though Shivaji crowned himself as the king, he did not fail to recognize the overwhelming power of the Mughals.

Shivaji was 44 years old when he got coronated. The towering fort of Raigadh became the capital. Shivaji ascended the golden throne after touching his mother's feet to seek her blessings. Gaga Bhatta held the golden umbrella over his head as a symbol of kingship and proclaimed that Shivaji had become the 'Chhatrapati'. Women offered '*aarti*'. Sages and saints blessed him. The assembled people shouted in great joy "Victory to Shivaji Maharaj!" The fort reverberated with the sound of the guns. He was acknowledged as an independent ruler by the Sultan of Bijapur and the English, who sent their well wishes through gifts.

On such an auspicious occasion, Samarth Ramdas sang in praise, "The land and its Dharma have been uplifted". A kingdom of peace was born.

The tiny kingdom established by Chhatrapati Shivaji, known as '*Hindavi Swaraja*' or the Sovereign Hindu state, grew and spread beyond Attock in Northwest India (now in Pakistan) and beyond Cuttack in East India. In due course of time, it became the strongest power in India.

June 1674, Shivaji was crowned king of the Marathas in a lavish Hindu ceremony at Raigad, by Gaga Bhatt

After the death of Chhatrapati Shivaji and his son, Sambhaji, their Prime Ministers or Peshwas became the real rulers. The Peshwas and the Maratha Sardars or chieftains like Shindes of Gwalior, Gaekwads of Baroda and Holkars of Indore contributed to the growth of the Maratha league.

CHAPTER 18
Shivaji - The Emperor

Shivaji could not rest even after establishing an independent kingdom. He undertook various reforms to promote the well being and safeguarded the interests of his subjects. He also made special provisions to take care of the safety and financial security of the soldiers who travel to far off lands during the times of war.

Shivaji had great love and sympathy for the poor farmers of villages, who groaned under the injustice of the wealthy zamindars. Shivaji took over the land of such zamindars and distributed them among the cultivators of the soil.

Shivaji also gave great importance to the field of education and literacy among its people. The glory of Sanskrit as a language was overshadowed due to the advent of Persian language. Shivaji worked and propagated the use of Sanskrit words instead of Persian words.

Shivaji was never superstitious. He discarded the belief that it was sinful to undertake a journey on the seas. In

fact, he undertook many journeys on seas to establish various forts in his kingdom.

Shivaji had made a record of building 160 forts in his lifetime. He built a unique fort 'Sindhudurga' on an island near Malvan. He laid the foundation of the fort by mixing concrete with molten lead. The stones used in the fort had worn out due to continuous attack of the ocean waves. He also built a few more sea forts, like Suvarnadurga, Padmadurga and Vijayadurga. These sea forts were used as shelters for his navy and also secured them from enemies who did not have a navy. This also helped to keep a check on the activities of the naval powers like the British, the Portuguese and the Abyssinians.

Shivaji despised the people who were corrupt and who worked against their country. He hated those who betrayed their motherland. He would not have flinched from punishing even his own son, if he had turned against his country. Shivaji was an embodiment of justice. He never bestowed any special favours to his relatives. He encouraged those who were virtuous and worthy and

made sure that they progressed and were promoted to high places. There was no place for selfishness in his kingdom. Shivaji always meted out severe punishment to those who disobeyed his orders. Likewise, Shivaji modified every aspect of his social and political life.

He stabilized the state with effective civil and military administration and adopted a policy of religious tolerance to accommodate all religions and sects in his state. He was the first Maratha Chhatrapati to start the Raj Shaka or the royal era and issued Shivarai, the gold coin, on the occasion of his coronation in 1674.

Shivaji made it a policy to never desecrate a mosque or seize women. This made it possible for Muslim men to serve his army. With the help of a larger force, Shivaji conquered the coastal places between Mumbai and Goa.

Whenever the enemy forces gravely threatened him, the crafty Shivaji would miraculously escape. This added to his stories of bravery and his legendary and undefeatable status as a king.

CHAPTER 19
The Reformer

Apart from the reforms mentioned in the previous chapters, Shivaji took up many other reforms as follows:

- Soon after ascending the throne, Shivaji stopped the use of Persian in his administration. He published a glossary of equivalent words with Sanskrit origin, called *Rajvyavahar Kosha*.
- Shivaji started cannon factories, a unique act in itself. Earlier, Hindu rulers used to buy cannons from the Portuguese, British or other Europeans. Later, Shivaji's son Sambhaji took a step further and started ordinance factories. Marathas, thereafter, produced both cannons and ammunitions.
- Shivaji imposed severe punishments for heinous crimes like rapes and disrespect to women, which included chopping of hands of the guilty.
- All the Indian kings, except Chandragupta, before and after Shivaji and his son followed the feudalist practice, whereby the king used to allocate a few villages or

towns to his knights. Under this system, the feudal lord maintained his own army and the revenue of the estate used to go entirely to his pocket. Thus, the Knights practiced loyalty to their own lands but not to the kingdom. Shivaji never gave such benefits to his knights. They were on the payroll of the government. Even the salary of the soldiers was paid by the Swarajya administration.

- Shivaji was the first Indian king to take up amphibious operations and jointly attack using cavalry, army and navy. After Raja Chola, he was the only king in India to

build up such a strong navy. He had formulated strict rules for the army, civil servants and authorities. He had stated in a letter to a General on the do's and don'ts for the army, "Even a thread of the length of a finger or even one coriander leaf stalk had to be bought by an official, failing which a penalty shall be imposed". Shivaji encouraged independent functioning of the judiciary which slashed the involvement of the executive wing.

- On the occasion of his coronation, Shivaji started a new calendar called *Rajashaka*.

CHAPTER 20
More Reforms

Shivaji was a great trainer and trained his team members' very well. He had a well designed administrative and military system. The reflection of the discipline and pride in his people along with the strength of his kingdom created history.

The Maratha power was the only kingdom in the world, which fought against Aurangzeb for seventeen years without a king. Aurangzeb had come to Maharashtra with a vow to destroy the Hindu kingdom of Marathas. He struggled for twenty-two years, but finally died in Maharashtra and could never return to Delhi. This reduced the mighty Mughal empire as a puppet in the hands of the Marathas. He followed the principles of Chanakya of '*Sama, Dama, Danda, Bheda*' to ensure victory for the Hindavi Swarajya.

During Shivaji's rule, Aurangzeb destroyed the Kashi Vishweshvar temple. Shivaji then vowed to pull down the mosque and rebuild the Vishweshvar temple. He had organized a highly capable army. His military genius is proved by his adaptation of the system of warfare. This system promised him victory irrespective of the races, nature of the country, weapon of the age and the internal condition of his enemies. His army was strong and invincible in the age of Aurangzeb.

He developed a well-coiled network of spies across India. With their help, he kept track of all the activities of the centre of power, whether Mughal, Adilshahi, Nizam, British, or Portuguese. Based on their leads, he used to strike his enemies in their weakest time and pace, which works to his advantage. The best example is his attack on Surat, which was the commercial capital of the Mughal Empire.

Shivaji stopped the practice of rewarding subjects with lands. Earlier, kings used to reward subjects with rights to

revenue, especially famous citizens or war heroes. These people would then act like local rulers, become a power centre and establish their own rule within the kingdom. Owning individual cavalry was banned by Shivaji. In his kingdom, all horses were property of the state.

He started the concept of Council of Ministers, the '*Ashta Pradhan Mandal*', where each minister was given the responsibility to handle one of the major departments of the administration. Their jobs were well-defined and necessary responsibility and authority was provided as required. Major decisions were made only when the members unanimously agreed and proper discussions were held within the Council. This system was different as compared to other standard durbars in India.

Shivaji's other achievements also included his rural reforms. He reintroduced a dual tax structure, depending on the condition and types of soil.

Shivaji intimately understood a farmer's life as he used to play with the lads of local farmers as a child and had seen their woes and joys closely.

As a ruler, he was always compassionate to his subjects and keen to help them in their problems. He improved the condition of the farmers by allowing taxes to be paid in kind, granted loans, and simplified the tax structure by imposing lower taxes on poor farmers. Such moves helped the poor subjects to free themselves from the clutches of the local moneylenders and landlords. Shivaji took up to maintain wells, lakes and construct water tanks, inns, temples and roads across his kingdom.

Shivaji stopped the practice of slavery and bonded labour, which was prevalent in India. The Europeans used to enslave Indian labourers and sell them to Africa, East Asia and South America. This used to happen with the support of local touts, who would do it at a very menial price. Shivaji imposed severe punishment on this trade. He also banned in-house slavery.

For Shivaji, the true nature of struggle was against the Mughals. His struggle indicated a rise of native power against a foreign power. It was not a struggle against religion, but a struggle against a powerful and unjust government. He fought against a power that was foreign in its ideology and which did not contribute in the well-being of the masses.

CHAPTER 21
Shivaji - The Man

Shivaji's private life reflected a higher standard of morality. He was a devoted son, loving father and an attentive husband. He was intensively spiritual and remained respectful to holy men throughout his lifetime. He was fond of listening to scripture readings, sacred songs and stories. He remained, throughout his life, strictly free from vice. Napoleon and Alexander were great rulers and

so were many other Indian kings and emperors, but none were free from vice. So, he was described by Guru Ramdas Swami as a '*rajayogi*'.

Shivaji had a charisma of a leader. He threw a spell over the people who knew him. He attracted the best elements of the country to his side and won the most

devoted service from officers. His dazzling victories and polite demeanor made him an idol among the soldiers. He had a unique skill of reading people's mind. He precisely tried to find people with best quality and character in the service of *swarajya*.

He had an extraordinary human resource management. He instilled pride and passion for the '*Hindavi Swarajya*' in each member of his team. The conditions from which he rose to sovereignty intensified the greatness of Shivaji as a genius.

An analysis of Shivaji's life highlights his expanding visions. Shivaji as a character emerged solely by his efforts and left a mark by creating a nation. He was responsible for releasing forces that changed the political map of India in the eighteenth century. Within 50 years of the death of Aurangzeb, the Marathas overran the entire subcontinent of India. They successfully took possession of a greater half of the country. It was only in 1803, when British took over the sovereignty of India.

CHAPTER 22
Successors of Shivaji

After Shivaji's death, two of his sons competed for the kingdom and Sambhaji was declared victorious. He continued to dislike Aurangzeb and always hindered his path. Sambhaji sheltered Prince Akbar, who was rebelling against his father. As fate would have it, Aurangzeb was drawn back to Deccan to chase his offending son. In 1982, the emperor and his staff moved to Deccan, never to return to Delhi. During a short reign of nine years Sambhaji (1657-1689), he dealt with a lot of feuds. In addition to domestic clashes, he was confronted with the Sindhis, the Portuguese and the Mughals. He was brutally murdered in 1689 by the Mughals which inspired a wave of patriotism in the Maratha region. The Marathas, under the leadership of his brother, Rajaram, waged a war of independence against the imperial army of Aurangzeb. Until his death in 1707, Aurangzeb struggled in vain to eradicate Maratha power. In 1700, Tarabai, Rajaram's widow, declared her son Shivaji II as Chhatrapati. But when in 1707, Sambhaji's son Shahu was released from

Mughal captivity and gained support from the Maratha elite, a civil war ensued in Maharashtra, and Tarabai set up a separate gadi or throne at Panhala in Kolhapur. In a palace revolution in 1714, Shivaji II was removed, Tarabai declared Sambhaji, the second son of Rajaram, as the Chhatrapati of Kolhapur, which Shahu finally recognized by the Treaty of Warna of 1731.

CHAPTER 23
Remembering Shivaji

Even after centuries of Shivaji's reign, people continue to pay tribute to the great warrior.

Remembering him, Pandit Jawaharlal Nehru said,

"Shivaji did not belong to Maharashtra alone; he belonged to the whole Indian nation. Shivaji was not an ambitious ruler anxious to establish a kingdom for himself but a patriot inspired by a vision and political ideas derived from the teachings of the ancient philosophers. He studied the merits and faults of the systems of administration in kingdoms existing at the time and determined his own policies and administration in the light of that knowledge."

"A devout Hindu, he was tolerant of other religions and established a number of endowments for maintaining sacred places belonging to them. As a general he was undoubtedly one of the greatest in Indian history; he saw the need for and raised a navy to guard his coastline and to fight against the British and the Dutch. Pratapgadh Fort built in 1656 stands even today, as a monument which accredits to his military genius.

"Shri Shivaji is a symbol of many virtues, more especially of love of country."

D. Kincaidszys in '*The Grand Rebel*' says,

"In spite of the character of a crusade which Ramdas's blessings gave to Shivaji's long struggle, it is remarkable how little religious animosity or intolerance Shivaji displayed. His kindness to Catholic priests is an agreeable contrast to the proscriptions of the Hindu priesthood in the Indian and Maratha territories of the Portuguese. Even his enemies remarked on his extreme respect for Mussulman priests, for mosques and for the Koran. The Muslim historian Khafi Khan, who cannot mention Shivaji in his chronicle without adding epithets of vulgar abuse, nevertheless acknowledges that Shivaji never entered a conquered town without taking measures to safeguard the

mosques from damage. Whenever a Koran came to his possession, he treated it with the same respect as if it had been one of the sacred works of his own faith. Whenever his men captured Mussulman ladies, they were brought to Shivaji, who looked after them as if they were his wards till he could return them to their relations."

Indira Gandhi said,

"I think Shivaji ranks among the greatest men of the world. Since we were a slave country, our great men have been somewhat played down in world history. Had the same person been born in a European country, he would have been praised to the skies and known everywhere. It would have been said that he had illumined the world."

CHAPTER 24
Timeline of Shivaji

The rise of Shivaji and the Marathas is an important factor in the history of India.

Shivaji(1627-1680 AD) was the founder of the Maratha kingdom. He was greatly inspired by the heroes of Hindu mythologies and he considered it his mission to liberate India from Islamic rulers.

Below is given a chronology of events in Shivaji's life:
- 1594: Birth of Shahaji Bhosale (Shivaji's father)
- 1596: Birth of Jijabai (Shivaji's mother)
- 1603: Marriage of Shahaji and Jijabai
- Feb 19, 1627: Shivaji is born on fort Shivneri
- 1630-1631: Famine in Maharashtra
- 1637: Shivaji arrives in Pune
- May 14, 1640: Marriage of Shivaji and Saibai
- April 15, 1645: Oath at Rohideshwar
- 1646: Shivaji captures Torana
- Oct 1648: Defeats Fateh Khan

- Jan 15, 1656: Javali won
- 1657: Sambhaji is born
- Nov 10, 1659: Shivaji kills Afzal Khan on Pratapgadh
- July 1660: Escape from Panhala - Death of Baji Prabhu Deshpande
- April 5, 1663: Night attack on Shaista Khan
- Jan 6-10, 1664: Raid on Surat
- Nov 15, 1664: Construction of Sindhudurg begins
- June 1665: Shivaji surrenders to Mirza Raje Jaisingh
- Sept 30, 1665: Aurangzeb's *farmaan* to Shivaji. Shivaji joins Mughals.
- Dec 1665: Netaji Palkar (Shivaji's right arm) joins Adil Shah.
- Jan 1666: Mughals suffer first defeat in Deccan at the hands of Adil Shah
- May 12, 1666: Aurangzeb and Shivaji come face to face at Delhi Darbar
- Aug 17, 1666: Escape from Agra
- Sept 2, 1666: Shivaji reaches Rajgad
- 1667: Bardesh campaign, truce with Portuguese. Death of Jaisingh.
- 1668: At the receiving end in Goa
- Sept 1669: Aurangazeb erases Kashi Vishweshvar Temple

- 1670: Nilopant captures Purandhar. Second raid on Surat
- 1672: Diler Khan raids Pune
- 1673: Panhala and Pratapgadh are captured
- Feb 24, 1674: Death of Prataprao Gujar
- June 6, 1674: Shivaji is crowned as the Chhatrapati Shivaji at Raigadh. Maratha Power is established.
- June 17, 1674: Death of Jijabai
- Dec 10, 1674: Campaign of Khandesh
- 1675: Mughals raid Kalyan-Bhivandi, Marathas win Karwar
- Aug 1676: Moropant Peshwa attacks Janjira
- June 19, 1676: Netaji Palkar returns
- Jan 1677: Defeats Husenkhan Miyana on Karnatak campaign
- March 1677: Meets Kutub Shah
- May 1677: Jinji is won by Marathas
- July 5, 1677: Sherkhan surrenders to Shivaji
- Aug 1677: Diler Khan replaces Bahadur Khan as the Chief of Mughals, in Deccan
- June 1678: Shivaji captures Gadag
- Dec 13, 1678: Sambhaji joins Diler Khan
- Feb 1679: Aurangzeb arrives in Aurangabad to wipe out Marathas

- Nov 1679: Sambhaji deserts Diler Khan and returns to Marathas
- Jan 1680: Truce with British
- April 3, 1680: Death of Shivaji

www.ingramcontent.com/pod-product-compliance
Lightning Source LLC
LaVergne TN
LVHW091317080426
835510LV00007B/529